Discussions with strangers

: What we should know about new people around us

Albert D. Edwards

TABLE OF CONTENT

Chapter 1

Know who's around you

I'm a normal independent person who makes all opinions by myself. I predicate my opinions on my suspicion. I suppose I know the people around me veritably well. Some people are secure, some are not. But we frequently dig our own holes by choosing and trusting the wrong people. Is it wrong to trust the wrong people, or is the world so cruel that everyone around me is disgusting? And should I be so hysterical , or should I close my viewing lens and trust the people around me? Are you ready to face the coming sting with the courage and determination to face the coming sting, and can you still smile from time to time after this surge of shame? Confused Who to believe in this world? Who should I calculate on?

These studies came to my mind and I was looking for answers to these questions. But I know that where there is a will, there is always a way. I eventually figured out how to suppose about these issues around me, this mystification in my head that eventually he crowned in the three golden rules

Rule# 1. Observe People Around You rightly

rather of fastening on how someone behaves toward you, concentrate on how this person behaves toward others. He may speak to you kindly because you may be of good social standing, but the real reality may be that he is just pretending to be nice in front of you. Regulators to advise when observing When somebody is too kind to you When someone cares too important for you When someone is always trying to be on your side If someone is too kind In short, be wise in judging people. You do not have the right to say effects like,' he betrayed me' or' I detest him'. It's simply his palm and your failure. Darwin formerly said" survival of the fittest". still, at least be apprehensive of your surroundings, If you do not want to play this dirty game.

 Rule# 2 Classify a person into two orders (musketeers, not fellows)

 To produce markers like" stylish friend", " stylish friend", etc., since there are only two orders he's No need to use your head.," just musketeers"," university musketeers"," work musketeers"," musketeers who stink", etc. Of course, you can also count your musketeers from this bracket. also you have to test people for their style. The person you interact with must be either a friend or anon-friend. still, you're testing him her gal, If not. Scrutinize the person for a while before accepting as a friend. But when you realize this is your friend, you should be ready to give your 200 to your friend. But if you suppose this isn't your friend, your coffers (time ,plutocrat, advice, etc.) to him her. Indeed Callidas said," Watering dry trees is a waste of time and water." Do not forget this adage moreover. You do not have to pay to maintain a auto you do not enjoy. So" not musketeers" is always like someone differently auto. It's like bad debt on the balance distance. No way suppose of taking out a loan with bad debt.

Rule# 3 Do not make too numerous rules

You came to Earth to do commodity good for humanity. They are not just then to make the rules. Flash back that rule 3 is for following rules 1 and 2. This rule should warn you when you get lost. Be a smart player. However, do not try to find an justification for that mistake, If you mis estimate someone and lose. I suggest you find the root cause of this error and prepare for another challenge. This world is cruel, fight. You're smart and can live like a king. When you come a freshman, you always come a guinea gormandizer to others, and they come smarter to exercise you and challenge you in this world. " Whether you are a loser or a winner, both conditions will motivate you to become strong. But no way be average it's an fable for lesser failure

Chapter 2

Types of people

Are you familiar with the behavior style DISC system? There are four main styles or types of behavior in this system. A quick look at each behavioral style preference can tell you a lot about people. Everyone needs to interact with others, so It's very important to understand. Understanding why others behave the way they do and what lies behind it opens up a world of possibilities. If you are in a sales position, learning DISC will greatly improve your sales skills and sales performance. DISC is invaluable if you want to get along with others. Simply understanding the basics of the DISC will radically change your life and career. If there are any new skills a person can acquire, the ability to interact with others is definitely at the top of the list.

DISC's foundations date back thousands of years. Hippocrates identified four temperaments, including:

Optimistic - Air - Enthusiastic and Outgoing (Me Now)

Calm - Water - Calm and compassionate (currently S)

Melancholic - Rustic - Detailed and understated (currently C)

At the beginning of the last century, American psychologist William Marston created a modern version of his four temperament prototypes in his 1928 book Emotions of Normal People. Marston's technology gained prominence in the 1940s when the US military adopted it for recruiting during World War II. Since then, DISC has been active all over the world. In modern usage, the four behavioral styles are identified as Dominance, Influence, Consistency, and Honesty, forming the acronym DISC. The most widely used assessment in the world, his DISC is of little use once you have a basic understanding of each of the four behavioral styles. Understanding these four opens up a whole new world of possibilities. I first discovered his DISC many years ago and started using it with my sales team. It quickly proved to be an invaluable tool for everyone in the company. When the people you work with understand the basics of behavioral style, communication across your organization improves. Recognizing the styles of others can help us learn to interact differently, greatly improving the way people communicate. "If you want to change your attitude, you have to start by changing your mind set." Mary AnneBefore we get into each episode, a few things you should know about DISC style. Learn All Four Styles, Not Just Your Style It is important to understand each of the four styles to understand where your style competes or complements other styles.

Everyone has at least one dominant style. Some have two or more primary styles, but usually one is more powerful than the other. Note that each person has a few of each of the four styles, to varying degrees. For example, I have a medium I style with a very high D style, a nearly as high C style, and a very low S style. My partner has a very high I style, a high D style, moderate C and S styles. If we didn't understand DISC in our lives, our actions are set towards many conflicts.

DISC is situational

As you do your DISC assessment, think about where you will benefit most: at work, at home, at church. Each of these attitudes can affect your behavioral preferences. So to get an accurate review, you'll have to pick where you plan to use it.Sure, some may be the same in all settings, but most aren't.

Let's look at each of the four main behavioral styles.

D – Dominance

It is estimated that approximately 3% of the population has a high-D behavioral style. D likes to be in control or in charge and challenges others. They tend to be straightforward, confident, and results-oriented.

An ineffective characteristic of D is when demanding, boastful, or sarcastic.

I — Influence

I'm about 11% of the population, so I've probably encountered more I's than D's in my lifetime. You are people-oriented, you love to talk, you are a good communicator, and you are persuasive. My ineffective traits include talking too much, being too enthusiastic, and not being able to concentrate.

S Stable

S are often team players in the world, making up about 69% of the total population. It's quite possible that you know some S in your life. S tend to be traditional, good listeners, loyal, consistent, supportive, and persistent. Your ineffective traits may include indecision, passiveness, over-tolerance, and resistance to change.

C — Conscience

About 17% of the population is made up of C. Most likely you know some C. They usually care about details such as precision and accuracy and are often critical thinkers. Ineffective traits include being overly perfectionist, detached, somewhat detached, and critical of themselves and others.

The table below provides a good way to think about the four styles. At the extremes of the x-axis (horizontal) are reserved and open, or task-oriented and people-oriented. The extrema of the (vertical) Y-axis are directly opposite Indirect or faster to a more moderate pace. Each extreme has its preferred style. For best results, we recommend using the DISC Assessment Service to take a quick 10-20 minute online test to determine your behavioral style. In the meantime, you can easily identify your preferences by looking at the table and asking a few simple questions.

Question 1

Look at the bottom and top of the chart, do you prefer to be less direct or more direct? Do you consider yourself fast-paced, or do you prefer taking things a bit slowly? Choose either bottom or top.

Question 2

Look at the left side and right side of the chart. Are you more reticent or more open? Do you prefer to work on one or farther tasks, or do you prefer to be with people? Choose left or right.

Must not belong to any of the four areas of the chart. As you can see, if you land up and left and down and right, your dominant style is presumably. Main style is presumably.

Its time to decides who you meet in life, your heart decides who you need in life, your conduct decide who stays around you says Anonymouspeaker.

Last Words

There is no lower price in life than getting along with other people, and Slice can help you achieve that. While the golden rule countries, " do unto others the way you would have them do unto you, " the Slice rule underlies that awful rule. Before a person may accept the golden rule, they constantly want you to do unto others the way they want to be done unto! When you learn to communicate in their favored style, their world, and your world changes. constantly drastically! The swish way to witness the benefits of using Slice in your life or at work is to consolidate your understanding of the basics outlined in this composition and to exercise them. Partake the composition with someone you are close to, do the quick assessment explained over, and begin to uncover the amazing benefits of knowledge to understand others more. I leave a final citation for you to consider There is no better test of a man's integrity than his responses when he is wrong, says Marvin Williams.

Chapter 3

How to get new friend

Research shows that making friends can be difficult and that millions of people are lonely. Here, four of his new connections explain how. Plus, psychologist Linda Blair has a tip. It's so easy when kids are on the playground, but the words "Will you be my friend?" are never heard by adults. Teenagers are full of easy-to-make (and sometimes forgettable) friendships when they're enthusiastic, outgoing, and energetic. And there are various demands in life such as engagement, marriage, moving, changing jobs, family, etc., and friendship is born from there. I love seeing my friends go through big moments in their lives, but sometimes I feel lonely because I value my friendships. Some friends are geographically far apart, others don't have much time, and no matter how hard you try, it's not easy to see each other as often as you like. According to a recent study conducted by the Red Cross in collaboration with her Co-op, her more than 9 million adults in the UK often or always feel lonely. We are facing an epidemic of loneliness, and Teresa May took the step earlier this year to appoint Tracy Crouch as her "secretary of loneliness". Loneliness is something we all experience to varying degrees from time to time, but it's also something we're reluctant to admit. It has been found to be associated with good health, happiness and happiness. However, making friends as an adult can be difficult and time consuming.

Last week, a University of Kansas study found that it takes two people 90 hours to become friends and 200 hours to become close friends. Clinical psychologist Linda Black agrees that this can be difficult to achieve: Usually the cornerstone of finding friends is sharing experiences. As is seldom the case, once these simple opportunities are over, you can forget about the first. The basis of friendship is similar passions or interests. Joining a group or class based on something you really love, or volunteering for something you care about, is a good first step toward making friends, she advises.Making new friends as an adult can be difficult, nerve-wracking at times, but also rewarding, 52-year-old Jacqueline Thomas happily shares. , when she moved in with her soon-to-retire partner David, she savored the opportunity to start fresh. We didn't know anyone here, so we had to start from down scratch. Now that our children have grown up, we have seen life a little quieter, but busier than before, Jacqueline introduced herself to her neighbors for the first time. She finds new friendships to be made by enrolling in various courses and groups at the community center. She reluctantly joined WI because she feared it would be all Jam and Jerusalem and I would be the youngest there. But she now says it was one of her best decisions of her life.

Don't be afraid to try something new, she emphasized. A lifelong wheelchair user, Jacqueline was intrigued by a poster promoting martial arts instruction in the parish hall.

After going through some doubts, she was surprised to find out how much she was enjoying it.

Now proudly holds a white belt in Shying Do Adapted Martial Arts. 'It just takes a piece of faith,' she says to make new connections instead of replacing old ones. Friendships are like onions, says Blair. Friends have all these layers, and the inner layer is your best friend— you've probably only had two or three in your entire life.At various stages, find can be positive. A personal success story stemmed from a friend's wedding last summer. Rebecca and I bond while we wait for the bride to move in. It turns out we live nearby in London and went to the same school in Dorset. (However, it was a different year when I was a child, but this is a crucial difference.) We discussed travel, food, and summer plans, but I wasn't sure our newfound friendship would last outside the tipsy haze of our wedding reception. Determined not to miss, I got her phone number.Fast forward to a meeting in a central London bar. I worried about what to wear if she would recognize me and if her awkward silence would last. But now they're staunch friends who explore the capital and take turns suggesting something new. Pete MacLeod found friendship when he joined a running club. Joining his local running and cycling groups was also a positive step. A great way to meet locals. A track and field fan and a member of my track and field club, Hercules Wimbledon, he's 25 and Pete McLeod agrees. After completing his master's degree at Loughborough University, he moved to Wimbledon for his first job and joined the club to keep himself fit. Making new good friends has been a grant: "It`s really satisfying. You get to exercise commodity you enjoy but also have the occasion to meet new people.' Pete made a New Year resolution in 2015 to push himself out of his comfort zone and speak to people more' The club was a good occasion to put that into practice when people aren t out of breath.' He counts some members of the sprinting group as veritably good musketeers now, with the japes and exchanges luring over into lawn tennis or walks and coffee at the weekend. It's important to be visionary, says Juliana Nabing, 42, who moved from Brazil to Chile with her hubby and two youthful children three times alone .' Don t sit and stay – it won t be. You have to laboriously search for new musketeers.' Now fluent in Spanish, she says that when she first moved she'd use the many words she knew to ask questions while staying for her children to finish at academy, indeed when she knew the answers' At first it was delicate because I really started to miss my musketeers and adult discussion, but the kiddies kept me busy and, through them, I made musketeers.' Juliana Nabing You have to laboriously search for musketeers. Now, via a Facebook group of English- speaking mums and her Spanish exchanges at the academy gates, she has a solid group of original and expat musketeers." The stylish thing is that you are old and do not judge people,' she says. Worst?' People do not know everything, so occasionally they do not understand your passions and your choices. You only have the pieces of the mystification.' gemütlichkeit can arise in unanticipated places. Stephen Walters, 43, and his family moved from Eday, a small Orkney islet of about 140 people, to the Orkney landmass. His woman Ronnie innovated Orkney Bequeens, the northernmost comber derby league in England. originally, Stephen trained as a adjudicator, where he was the only man, but he came a trainer despite having little experience in skating. Within a time, he says, he'd made numerous musketeers of all periods. The spirit of inclusivity and equivalency of the Roller Derby was a big draw to him, He admits that he has no way played sports much. Amy Perrin, author of the Bristol- grounded charity Marmalade Trust. to feel lonely? Meet people who have plodded with extreme insulation and set up happiness keep reading Embracing fellowship as an grown-up can be shocking, instigative, satisfying, and grueling . Taking a vault of faith can lift you up and get the ballrolling.Before you rush to your autumn martial trades class, she offers some simple but effective advice.

Linda Black's Friendship Tips

Build Trust

 Loving yourself before looking for musketeers is an important step in erecting a healthy relationship.

Find your passion, still

Take language classes, if you love nature, If you love languages.

Let's go out

Flash back, you did not adventure, and you did not get anything.' Just because you meet someone and it does not suit your fellowship does not mean you lose.

Meet in a Neutral position

Choose a neutral public space when you take the first step and move to a meeting outside of the original terrain in which you established a connection. This relieves the pressure that home hosting can bring, for illustration, and gives you time to concentrate on each other. Do not Anticipate Too important A common mistake is to anticipate too much from people. It's more realistic and healthier to have different musketeers for different reasons.

Chapter 4

Tools and strategies for good relationship

 Having good musketeers who love and support you for who you're is really important to your happiness. Learn what makes a good friend and how they can be there for you when they need you most.

* This is useful when you aren't sure about fellowship

*you do not know what to do or what to say to a friend

* They want to know what a good friend is and how to come

a good friend. Boys and girls dancing at a gig

* Why Good musketeers Are So Important

 Studies show that the advanced the quality of your connections, the more likely you're to be happy. Having a friend who's someone's good friend and has your reverse is good for your health, But what exactly makes a good friend?

Signs of a Good Friend

 musketeers come and go in your life. Anyhow of how long the fellowship lasts, the most important thing is that your friend accepts you. Good musketeers keep their pledges and show that they watch about themselves in lesser or lower ways.

 Good Friend will forever be by your side in whatever situation,

 do not judge you He will not bring you down or designedly hurt your passions kind and regardful to you someone you enjoy being with Pious secure and willing to tell the verity, indeed if it's hard to hear laugh with you keep it up when effects get tough. make you smile are you there to hear Comfort him when he cry. how to be a good friend still, you are formerly a good friend to them, If you treat your fellow humans in the ways described above. But knowing how to be there for your musketeers is not always easy. Hear to them Try to understand the state from your friend's sight. Ask questions to get a sense for the problem or problem, but the main thing is to hear to them. You do not have to know all the answers. Also, do not assume your friend needs advice. Your friend may just want to talk so you can find out for yourself. Get the data still, a good way to offer support is to know they've been diagnosed, If a friend has

a medical or internal health problem. Ask them what they need still, ask them what they need, If you are upset about someone and want to be there for them.

That way they know what can help them in tough times and you can support them in ways that are really helpful. still, ask your musketeers if it's okay to clinch them, If you like leverages. Give a thumb up and clinch! Hugging a friend is a great way to show that you watch about them. Physical contact can be comforting, especially when someone is feeling lonely.

Keep in touch

Indeed if you do not live hard, let your musketeers know you are there by staying in regular contact via social media, texting, or calling. convey passions You do not have to do much all the time, But just telling someone how important they're to you can make a big difference. Alright, let's go! Prepare to make a tough call, still you may need to act without their concurrence and seek their help, If you feel that your friend's safety is in peril. It can be a delicate decision, especially if you are upset about the other person's response.

What can I do now? Get tips on how to come a better listener. Want to sputter with a coworker who'll hear and help? Bespeak a free textbook- grounded session on Reach Out Peer Chat. Find out what you can do about poisonous gemütlichkeit.

Chapter 5

Living psychology

Friendships can have a huge impact on your health and well-being, but they are not always easy to develop and maintain. Understand what you can do to nurture and maintain it. What are the benefits of friendship? Good friends are good for your health. Friends celebrate the good times and support you in the bad. Friends prevent isolation and loneliness and give us the opportunity to provide much-needed company. Friends can also:

Increase a sense of belonging and purpose

Increase happiness and reduce stress

improve self-confidence and self-esteem

Helps cope with trauma such as divorce, serious illness, job loss, and death of the loved ones, Encouraging changes or avoidance of unhealthy lifestyle habits such as excessive drinking and sedentary lifestyles , Friends also play an important role in promoting overall health. Adults with strong social ties have a lower risk of many serious health problems, including depression, high blood pressure, and an unhealthy body mass index (BMI). In fact, research shows that older adults who have meaningful connections and social support are more likely to live longer than their less connected peers. Finding friends and maintaining friendships can be difficult ,Why? Many adults find it difficult to make new friends or keep existing ones. Friendships can take a backseat to other priorities such as work, taking care of children, and aging parents. You and your friends may have drifted apart due to changes in your life or interests. Or you may have moved to a new community and haven't found a way to meet people yet. Building and maintaining good friendships takes effort. But the joy and comfort that friendship brings is worth the investment. How many healthy friends do you have? Quality is more important than quantity. Maintaining a diverse network of friends and acquaintances is good, but building close and meaningful relationships can help you feel a greater sense of belonging and happiness. What opportunities do you have to make new friends? It is possible to form friendships with people who are already on your social network. Think of someone you've interacted with casually and made a positive impression. You can make new friends and nurture existing relationships:

 Reunion with an old friend

 Reach out to people you've had fun chatting with at social gatherings

 Introduce a neighbor

Make time to connect with family

If you remember someone you would like to know more about, please contact them. Ask a mutual friend or acquaintance to share the person's contact information or reintroduce them via text her messages, emails, or personal visits. Invite them for meal To meet new people who you might want to be friends with, you have to go to places where other people gather. Don't limit him to one strategy for meeting people. The wider the effort, the greater the chance of success. Patience is also important. Instead of waiting for an invitation to keep trying, take the initiative. You may have to propose your plans a few times before deciding whether your new friend's interest is mutual. Try out some of these ideas. For example: Participate in regional events. Find groups and clubs that share common interests and hobbies. These groups can be found online. They may also be posted in newspapers or on community bulletin boards. There are also many websites that help you connect with new friends in your neighborhood or town. Do a Google search using terms such as [your city] + social networks or [your neighborhood] + meet ups. Volunteer. Donate your time or talents to hospitals, places of worship, museums, community centers, charities, or other organizations. Working with people who share common interests can help you build strong connections. Create and accept an invitation. Invite friends over for coffee or lunch. If you are invited to a social gathering, say yes. Give back by reaching out to people who recently invited you to an activity. take a new interest Join college and community education classes to meet people with similar interests. Take a class at your local gym, senior center, or community fitness facility, Join a faith group, Take advantage of special activities and introductory events for new members. Go for a walk Take your children and pets outside. Chat with neighbors who are traveling or visiting your favorite park and start a conversation there. Above all, stay positive. You may not be friendly to everyone you meet, but maintaining a friendly demeanor and attitude can improve your relationships in life. You can also sow the seeds of friendship with new acquaintances. How does social media affect friendships? Participating in chat groups and online communities can help you make and maintain connections and feel less lonely. However, research shows that the use of social networking sites does not necessarily lead to larger offline networks or closer offline relationships with network members. Also, remember to be careful when giving out personal information or arranging activities with people you've only met online. How can I maintain friendships? Building and maintaining friendships requires give and take. You can be a supporter or a recipient. You can strengthen your bond by letting your friends know that you care and appreciate them. Having good friends is just as important to you as it is to surround yourself with good friend .coffee or lunch.

How to Build Friendships:

Be friendly; This most basic behavior remains at the heart of any successful relationship. Think of friendships as emotional bank accounts. All kind gestures and gratitude are credited to this account, while criticism and negative comments are deducted from the account. be a good audience. Ask what's going on in your friend's life. Eye contact, body language, and the occasional short comment like "That sounds like fun" let them know you're paying attention. Be empathetic when your friend recounts hard times or difficult experiences, but don't offer advice unless the friend asks for it. Open. Build intimacy with your friends by being open about yourself.Being willing to share personal experiences and concerns shows that your friend holds a special place in your life, which can deepen your connection. Show that you can be trusted. To build a strong friendship, it is important to be responsible, dependable, and trustworthy. Keep your promises and arrive on time. Keep your promises to your friends. If your friend shares sensitive information, keep it private. Make yourself available. It takes time to build a close friendship - together. Make an effort to meet new friends regularly and check in between meetings. The first few calls or meetings may feel uncomfortable, but as you become more comfortable with each other, that feeling will dissipate. Manage your nerves with mindfulness.

Imagining the worst possible social situation may make you want to stay home. Use Mindfulness practices to reshape your thinking. Every time you imagine the worst, Notice how often the embarrassing situation you fear actually happens. You may find that the scenarios you fear don't usually happen. When an embarrassing situation arises, remember that your emotions will pass and you can deal with it until then. Yoga and other mind and body relaxation practices can also help reduce anxiety and help you cope with stressful situations. It is never too late to generate new friends or reconnect with old ones you had. Investing time in making friends and developing friendships can result in better health and prospects for years to come.

9 798849 810256